UNION
AND
COMMUNION
WITH CHRIST

UNION
AND
COMMUNION
WITH CHRIST

J. Hudson Taylor

BETHANY HOUSE PUBLISHERS
MINNEAPOLIS, MINNESOTA 55438
A Division of Bethany Fellowship, Inc.

FOREWORD

This little book, whose design is to lead the devout Bible student into the green pastures of the Good Shepherd, thence to the banqueting house of the King, and thence to the service of the vineyard, is one of the abiding legacies of Hudson Taylor to the church. In the power of an evident unction from the Holy One, he has been enabled herein to unfold in simplest language the deep truth of the believer's personal union with the Lord, which under symbol and imagery is the subject of the Song of Songs. And in so doing he has ministered an unfailing guidance to one of the most commonly neglected and misunderstood of the sacred Scriptures. For how many have said in bewilderment at the richness of language and profusion of figure which both conceal and reveal its meaning, "How can I understand except some man should guide me?" It is safe to say that these pages cannot fail to help and bless all such.

To those who knew him, Hudson Taylor's life was in the nature of emphasis upon the

value of this small volume. For what he
here expounds he also exemplified. If his
words indicate the possibility and blessedness of union with Christ, his whole life de-
clared it in actual experience. He lived as
one who was "married to another, even to
him who is raised from the dead," and as
the outcome of that union he brought forth
fruit unto God. What he *was* has given a
meaning and confirmation to what he has
here *said*, which cannot be exaggerated, It
is inevitable that there are those who will
read and reject, as mystical and imprac-
tical, that which is so directly concerned
with the intimacies of fellowship with the
unseen Lord. I would, however, venture to
remind such that the writer of these pages
founded the China Inland Mission! He trans-
lated his vision of the Beloved into life-
long strenuous service, and so kept it un-
dimmed through all the years of a life which
has had hardly a parallel in these our days.

This is really the commendation of the
following short chapters. They proclaim an
Evangel which has been distilled from experience, and form at least a track through
this fenced portion of God's Word, which
will lead many a one who treads it into the
joys of Emmanuel's land.

J. J. Stuart Holden

TABLE OF CONTENTS

THE SONG OF SOLOMON

Introduction

The great purpose toward which all the dispensational dealings of God are tending is revealed to us in I Corinthians 15:28, "That God may be all in all." With this agrees the teaching of our Lord in John 17:3: "And this is [the object of] life eternal, that they might know thee the only true God, and Jesus Christ, whom thou has sent." This being so, shall we not act wisely by keeping this object ever in view in our daily life and study of God's holy Word?

All Scripture is given by inspiration of God and is profitable, and hence no part is, or can be, neglected without loss. Few portions of the Word will help the devout student more in the pursuit of this all-important knowledge of God than the much-neglected Song of Solomon. Like other portions of the Word of God, this book has its difficulties. But so have all the works of God. Is not the fact that they surpass our unaided powers of comprehension and research a finger that points to their divine origin? Can feeble man expect to grasp

divine power, or to understand and inter-
pret the works or the providences of the
All-wise? And if not, is it surprising that
His Word also needs superhuman wisdom
for its interpretation? Thanks be to God,
the illumination of the Holy Ghost is prom-
ised to all who seek for it: what more can
we desire?

Read without the key, this book is specially unintelligible, but that key is easily
found in the express teachings of the New
Testament. The Incarnate Word is the true
key to the written Word; but even before
the Incarnation, the devout student of the
Old Testament would have found much help
to the understanding of the sacred mysteries of this book in the prophetic writings,
for there Israel was taught that her Maker
was her Husband. John the Baptist, the
last of the prophets, recognized the Bridegroom in the person of Christ, and said,
"He that hath the bride is the bridegroom:
but the friend of the bridegroom, which
standeth and heareth him, rejoiceth greatly
because of the bridegroom's voice: this my
joy therefore is fulfilled." Paul in the fifth
chapter of Ephesians goes still further, and
teaches that the union of Christ with His
church, and her subjection to Him, under-
lies the very relationship of marriage, and

affords the pattern for every godly union.

In Solomon, the bridegroom king as well as author of this poem, we have a type of our Lord, the true Prince of Peace, in His coming reign. Then will be found not merely His bride, the church, but also a willing people, His subjects, over whom He shall reign gloriously. Then distant potentates will bring their wealth, and will behold the glory of the enthroned King, proving Him with hard questions, as once came the Queen of Sheba to King Solomon, and blessed will they be to whom this privilege is accorded. A brief glance will suffice them for a lifetime, but what shall be the royal dignity and blessedness of the risen and exalted bride! Forever with her Lord, forever like her Lord, forever conscious that His desire is toward her, she will share alike His heart and His throne. Can a study of the book which helps us to understand these mysteries of grace and love be other than most profitable?

It is interesting to notice the contrast between this book and that preceding it. The Book of Ecclesiastes teaches emphatically that "vanity of vanities, all is vanity," and is thus the necessary introduction to the Song of Solomon, which shows how true blessing and satisfaction are to be possessed. In like manner our Saviour's teaching in John 4 points out in word the powerlessness of earthly things to give lasting satisfaction, in striking contrast with the flow of blessing that results from the presence of the Holy Spirit—whose work it is, not to reveal Himself but Christ as the Bridegroom of the soul. "Whosoever drinketh of this water shall thirst again: but whosoever drinketh of the water that I shall give him shall never thirst; but the water that I shall give him shall be in him a well of water springing up [overflowing, on and on] unto everlasting life" (John 4:13-14).

We shall find it helpful to consider the book in six sections:

I. The Unsatisfied Life and Its Remedy (1:2—2:7).

II. Communion Broken—Restoration (2:8—3:5).

III. Unbroken Communion (3:6—5:1).

IV. Communion Again Broken—Restoration (5:2—6:10).

V. Fruits of Recognized Union (6:11—8:4).

VI. Unrestrained Communion (8:5-14).

In each of these sections we shall find the speakers to be the bride, the Bride-

groom, and the daughters of Jerusalem.
It is not usually difficult to ascertain the
speaker, though in some of the verses different conclusions have been arrived at.
The bride speaks of the Bridegroom as "her
Beloved," the Bridegroom speaks of her
as His "love," while the address of the
daughters of Jerusalem is more varied. In
the first four sections they style her as
the fairest among women, but in the fifth
she is spoken of as the Shulamite, or the
King's bride, and also as the Prince's
daughter.

The student of this book will find great
help in suitable Bible marking. A horizontal
line marking off the address of each speaker, with a double line to divide the sections,
would be useful, as also a system of vertical
lines in the margin to indicate the speaker.
We have ourselves ruled a single line to
connect the verses which contain the utterances of the bride, a double line to indicate
those of the Bridegroom, and a waved line
to indicate the addresses of the daughters
of Jerusalem.

It will be observed that the bride is the
chief speaker in Sections One and Two,
and is much occupied with herself; but in
Section Three, where the communion is unbroken, she has little to say, and appears

as the hearer; the daughters of Jerusalem give a long address, and the Bridegroom His longest. In that section for the first time He calls her His bride, and allures her to fellowship in service. In Section Four the bride again is the chief speaker, but after her restoration the Bridegroom speaks at length, and "upbraideth not." In Section Five, as we noticed, the bride is no longer called "the fairest among women," but claims herself to be, and is recognized as, the royal bride. In Section Six the Bridegroom claims her from her very birth, and not merely from her espousals, as God in Ezekiel 16 claimed Israel.

> In the secret of His presence
>   How my soul delights to hide!
> Oh, how precious are the lessons
>   Which I learn at Jesus' side!
> Earthly cares can never vex me,
>   Neither trials lay me low;
> For when Satan comes to vex me,
>   To the secret place I go!

THE SONG OF SOLOMON

The Title

"The Song of Songs, which is Solomon's."

Well may this book be called *the* Song of Songs! There is no song like it. Read aright, it brings a gladness to the heart which is as far beyond the joy of earthly things as heaven is higher than the earth. It has been well said that this is a song which grace alone can teach, and experience alone can learn. Our Saviour, speaking of the union of the branch with the vine, adds, "These things have I spoken unto you, that my joy might remain in you, and that your joy might be full" (John 16:11). And the beloved disciple, writing of Him who was from the beginning, who was with the Father, and was manifested unto us, in order that we might share the fellowship which He enjoyed, also says, "These things write we unto you, that your joy may be full." Union with Christ, and abiding in Christ—what do they not secure? Peace, perfect peace; rest, constant rest; answers to all our prayers; victory

over all our foes; pure, holy living; ever-
increasing fruitfulness. All, all of these are
the glad outcome of abiding in Christ. To
deepen this union, to make more constant
this abiding, is the practical use of this
precious Book.

SECTION I

The Unsatisfied Life and Its Remedy

Song of Solomon 1:2—2:7

There is no difficulty in recognizing the bride as the speaker in verses 2-7. The words are not those of one dead in trespasses and sins, to whom the Lord is as a root out of a dry ground—without form and comeliness. The speaker has had her eyes opened to behold His beauty, and longs for a fuller enjoyment of His love.

Let Him kiss me with the kisses of His mouth:
For Thy love[1] is better than wine.

It is well that it should be so; it marks a distinct stage in the development of the life of grace in the soul. And this recorded experience gives, as it were, a divine warrant for the desire for perceptible manifestations of His presence—perceptible communications of His love. It was not always so with her. Once she was contented in His absence—other society and other occupations sufficed her—but now it can never

---

[1] Loves; i.e., endearments, caresses.

be so again. The world can never be to
her what it once was. The betrothed bride
has learned to love her Lord, and no other
society than His can satisfy her. His visits
may be occasional and may be brief, but
they are precious times of enjoyment. Their
memory is cherished in the intervals, and
their repetition longed for. There is no real
satisfaction in His absence, and yet, alas,
He is not always with her: He comes and
goes. Now her joy in Him is a heaven below,
then again she is longing, and longing in
vain, for His presence. Like the ever changing tide, her experience is an ebbing and
flowing one. It may even be that unrest
is the rule, satisfaction the exception.

Is there no help for this? Must it always
continue so? Has He, can He have created
these unquenchable longings only to tanta-
lize them? Strange indeed it would be if
this were the case. Yet are there not many
of the Lord's people whose habitual experience corresponds with hers? They know
not the rest, the joy of abiding in Christ,
and they know not how to attain to it, nor
why it is not theirs. Are there not many
who look back to the delightful times of
their first espousals, who, so far from finding richer inheritance in Christ than they
then had, are even conscious that they have

lost their first love, and might express their experience in the sad lament:

> Where is the blessedness I knew
> When first I saw the Lord?

Others, again, who may not have lost their first love, may yet be feeling that the occasional interruptions to communion are becoming more and more unbearable, as the world becomes less and He becomes more. His absence is an ever-increasing distress: " 'Oh that I knew where I might find him!' . . . 'Let Him kiss me with the kisses of His mouth: for thy love is better than wine.' Would that His love were strong and constant like mine, and that He never withdrew the light of His countenance!"

Poor mistaken one! There is a love far stronger than thine waiting, longing for satisfaction. The Bridegroom is waiting for thee all the time, and the conditions that debar His approach are all of thine own making. Take the right place before Him, and He will be most ready, most glad, to "satisfy thy deepest longings, to meet, supply thine every need."

What should we think of a betrothed one whose conceit and self-will prevented not only the consummation of her own joy, but of his who had given her his heart? Though never at rest in his absence, she

cannot trust him fully, and she does not
care to give up her own name, her own
rights and possessions, her own will to him
who has become necessary for her happi-
ness. She would fain claim him fully, without giving up herself fully to him.

But this can never be: while she retains
her own name, she can never claim his.
She may not promise to love and honor
if she will not also promise to obey, and
until her love reaches that point of surrender she must remain an unsatisfied
lover—until then she cannot, as a satisfied
bride, find rest in the home of her husband.
While she retains her own will and the con-
trol of her own possessions she must be
content to live on her own resources—she
cannot claim his.

Could there be a sadder proof of the
extent and reality of the fall of man than
the deep-seated distrust of our loving Lord
and Master which makes us hesitate to
give ourselves entirely up to Him, which
fears that He might require something beyond our powers, or call for something that
we should find it hard to give or to do?
The real secret of an unsatisfied life lies
too often in an unsurrendered will.

And yet how foolish, as well as how
wrong, this is! Do we fancy that we are

wiser than He? or that our love for ourselves is more tender and strong than His? or that we know ourselves better than He does? How our distrust must grieve and wound afresh the tender heart of Him who was for us the Man of Sorrows!

What would be the feelings of an earthly bridegroom if he discovered that his bride-elect was dreading to marry him, lest, when he had the power, he should render her life insupportable? Yet how many of the Lord's redeemed ones treat Him just so! No wonder they are neither happy nor satisfied!

But true love cannot be stationary: it must either decline or grow. Despite all the unworthy fears of our poor hearts, divine love is destined to conquer. The bride exclaims:

> Thine ointments have a goodly fragrance;
> Thy name is as ointment poured forth;
> Therefore do the virgins love thee.

There was no such ointment as that with which the high priest was anointed: our Bridegroom is a priest as well as a king. The trembling bride cannot wholly dismiss her fears, but the unrest and the longing become unbearable and she determines to surrender all, and come what may to follow fully. She will yield her very self to Him, heart and hand, influence and possessions. Nothing can be so insupportable as His absence! If He lead to another Moriah, or even to a Calvary, she will follow Him.

Draw me: we will run after thee!

But ah! what follows? A wondrously glad surprise. No Moriah, no Calvary; on the contrary, a King! When the heart submits, then Jesus reigns. And when Jesus reigns, there *is* rest.

And where does He lead His bride?

The King hath brought me into his chambers.

Not first to the banqueting house—that will come in due season—but first to be alone with Himself.

How perfect! Could we be satisfied to meet a beloved one only in public? No, we want to take him aside—to have him all to ourselves. So with our Master: He takes His now fully consecrated bride aside, to taste and enjoy the sacred intimacies of His wondrous love. The Bridegroom of His church longs for communion with His people more than they long for fellowship with Him, and often has to cry:

Let me see thy countenance, let me hear
    thy voice;
For sweet is thy voice, and thy countenance
    is comely.

Are we not all too apt to seek Him because of our need rather than for His joy and pleasure? This should not be. We do not admire selfish children who only think of what they can get from their parents, and are unmindful of the pleasure that they may give or the service that they may render. But are not we in danger of forgetting that pleasing God means giving Him pleasure? Some of us look back to the time when the words "to please God" meant no more than not to sin against Him, not to grieve Him. But would the love of earthly parents be satisfied with the mere absence of disobedience? Or a bridegroom, if his bride only sought him for the supply of her own need?

A word about the morning watch may not be out of place here. There is no time so profitably spent as the early hour given to Jesus only. Do we give sufficient attention to this hour? If possible, it should be redeemed. Nothing can make up for it. We must take time to be holy!

One other thought: when we bring our questions to God, do we not sometimes either go on to offer some other petition, or leave the closet without waiting for replies? Does not this seem to show little expectation of an answer, and little desire

for one? Should we like to be treated so?
Quiet waiting before God would save from
many a mistake and from many a sorrow.

We have found the bride making a glad
discovery of a King—her King—and not a
cross, as she expected. This is the first-fruit
of her consecration.

> We will be glad and rejoice in thee,
> We will make mention of thy love more
>   than of wine:
> Rightly do they love thee.

Another discovery no less important
awaits her. She has seen the face of the
King, and, as the rising sun reveals that
which was hidden in the darkness, so His
light has revealed her blackness to her.
"Ah," she cries, "I am black!" "But comely," interjects the Bridegroom, with inimit-
able grace and tenderness. "Nay, black
as the tents of Kedar," she continues. "Yet
to Me," He responds, "thou art comely
as the curtains of Solomon!"

Nothing humbles the soul like sacred
and intimate communion with the Lord;
yet there is a sweet joy in feeling that
He knows *all*, and, notwithstanding, loves
us still. Things once called little negligences
are now seen with new eyes in the secret
of His presence. There we see the mistake,
the sin of not keeping our own vineyard.

This the bride confesses:

> Look not upon me, because I am swarthy,
> Because the sun hath scorched me.
> My mother's sons were incensed against me,
> They made me keeper of the vineyards;
> But mine own vineyard have I not kept.

Our attention is here drawn to a danger which is pre-eminently one of this day: the intense activity of our times may lead to zeal in service, *to the neglect of personal communion*. Such neglect will not only lessen the value of the service, but will also tend to incapacitate us for the highest service. If we are watchful over the souls of others, and neglect our own—if we are seeking to remove motes from our brother's eye, unmindful of the beam in our own, we shall often be disappointed with our powerlessness to help our brethren, while our Master will not be less disappointed in us. Let us never forget that what we are is more important than what we do, and that all fruit borne when not abiding in Christ must be fruit of the flesh and not of the Spirit. As wounds when healed often leave a scar, so the sin of neglected communion may be forgiven and yet the effect remain permanently.

We now come to a very sweet evidence of the reality of the heart-union of the bride

with her Lord. She is one with the Good
Shepherd: her heart at once goes instinc-
tively forth to the feeding of the flock; but
she would tread in the footsteps of Him
whom her soul loveth, and would neither
labor alone, nor in other companionship
than His own:

> Tell me, O thou whom my soul loveth,
> Where thou feedest thy flock, where thou
>   makest it to rest at noon:
> For why should I be as one that is veiled
> Beside the flocks of thy companions?

She will not mistake the society of His
servants for that of their Master.

> If thou know not, O thou fairest among
>   women,
> Go thy way forth by the footsteps of the flock,
> And feed thy kids beside the shepherds' tents.

These are the words of the daughters
of Jerusalem, and give a correct reply to
her questionings. Let her show her love
to her Lord by feeding His sheep, by caring
for His lambs (see John 21:15-17), and she
need not fear to miss His presence. While
sharing with other undershepherds in caring for His flock she will find the Chief
Shepherd at her side, and enjoy the tokens
of His approval. It will be service *with*
Jesus as well as *for* Jesus.

But far sweeter than the reply of the

daughters of Jerusalem is the voice of the
Bridegroom, who now speaks Himself. It
is the living fruit of her heart-oneness with
Him that makes His love break forth in
the joyful utterances of verses 9-11. For
it is not only true that our love for our
Lord will show itself in feeding His sheep,
but that He who when on earth said, "Inas-
much as ye have done it unto one of the
least of these my brethren, ye have done
it unto me," has His own heart-love stirred,
and not infrequently specially reveals Himself to those who are ministering for Him.

The commendation of the bride in verse
9 is one of striking appropriateness and
beauty:

> I have compared thee, O my love,
> To a company of horses in Pharaoh's chariots.

It will be remembered that horses orig-
inally came out of Egypt, and that the pure
breed still found in Arabia was during Solomon's reign brought by his merchants for
all the kings of the East. Those selected
for Pharaoh's own chariot would not only
be of the purest blood and perfect in propor-
tion and symmetry, but also perfect in
training, docile and obedient; they would
know no will but that of the charioteer,
and the only object of their existence would

be to carry the king wherever he would go. So should it be with the church of Christ: one body with many members, indwelt and guided by one Spirit; holding the Head, and knowing no will but His. Her rapid and harmonious movement should cause His kingdom to progress throughout the world.

Many years ago a beloved friend, returning from the East by the overland route, made the journey from Suez to Cairo in the cumbrous stagecoach then in use. The passengers on landing took their places, about a dozen wild young horses were harnessed with ropes to the vehicle, the driver took his seat and cracked his whip, and the horses dashed off, some to the right, some to the left, and others forward, causing the coach to start with a bound, and as suddenly to stop, with the effect of first throwing those sitting in the front seat into the laps of those sitting behind, and then of reversing the operation. With the aid of sufficient Arabs running on each side to keep these wild animals progressing in the right direction the passengers were jerked and jolted, bruised and shaken, until, on reaching their destination, they were too wearied and sore to take the rest they so much needed.

Is not the church of God today more like these untrained steeds than a company of horses in Pharaoh's chariot? And while self-will and disunion are apparent in the church, can we wonder that the world still lieth in the wicked one, and that the great heathen nations are barely touched?

Changing His simile, the Bridegroom continues:

> Thy cheeks are comely with plaits of hair,
> Thy neck with strings of jewels.
> We will make thee plaits of gold
> With studs of silver.

The bride is not only beautiful and useful to her Lord, but she is also adorned, and it is His delight to add to her adornments. Nor are His gifts perishable flowers, or trinkets destitute of intrinsic value: the finest of the gold, the purest of the silver, and the most precious and lasting of the jewels are the gifts of the Royal Bridegroom to His spouse; and these, plaited into her own hair, increase His pleasure who has bestowed them.

In verses 12-14 the bride responds:

> While the King sat at his table
> My spikenard sent forth its fragrance.

It is His presence and through His grace that whatever of fragrance or beauty may

be found in us comes forth. Of Him as
its source, through Him as its instrument,
and to Him as its end, is all that is gracious
and divine. But *He Himself* is better far
than all that His grace works in us.

> My beloved is unto me as a bundle of myrrh,
> That lieth betwixt my breasts.
> My beloved is unto me as a cluster of henna-
>   flowers
> In the vineyards of En-gedi.

Well is it when our eyes are filled with
His beauty and our hearts are occupied
with Him. In the measure in which this
is true of us we shall recognize the correla-
tive truth that His great heart is occupied
with us. Note the response of the Bridegroom:

> Behold, thou art fair, my love; behold, thou
>   art fair;
> Thine eyes are as dove's.

How can the Bridegroom truthfully use
such words of one who recognizes herself
as "black as the tents of Kedar"? And
still more strong are the Bridegroom's
words in 4:7:

> Thou art all fair, my love;
> And there is no spot in thee.

We shall find the solution of this difficulty in II Corinthians 3. Moses in contem-

plation of the Divine glory became so transformed that the Israelites were not able to look on the glory of his countenance. "We all, with unveiled face [beholding and] reflecting as a mirror the glory of the Lord, are transformed into the same image from glory to glory [*i.e.,* the brightness caught from His glory transforms us to glory], even as from the Lord the Spirit." Every mirror has two surfaces. The one is dull and unreflecting, and is all spots; but when the reflecting surface is turned fully toward us we see no spot, we see our own image. So while the bride is delighting in the beauty of the Bridegroom, He beholds His own image in her. There is no spot in that: it is all fair. May we ever present this reflection to His gaze, and to the world in which we live for the very purpose of reflecting Him.

Note again His words:

Thine eyes are as dove's,

or

Thou hast dove's eyes.

The hawk is a beautiful bird, and has beautiful eyes, quick and penetrating; but the Bridegroom desires not hawk's eyes in His bride. The tender eyes of the innocent dove are those which He admires. It was as a dove that the Holy Spirit came upon Him at His baptism, and the dove-like character is that which He seeks for in each of His people.

The reason why David was not permitted to build the temple was a very significant one. His life was far from perfect; and his mistakes and sins have been faithfully recorded by the Holy Spirit. They brought upon him God's chastenings, yet it was not any of these that disqualified him from building the temple, but rather his warlike spirit; and this though many of his battles, if not all, were for the establishment of God's Kingdom and the fulfillment of His promises to Abraham, Isaac, and Jacob. Solomon, the Prince of Peace, alone could build the temple. If we would be soul-winners and build up the church, which is His temple, let us note this: not by discussion nor by argument, but by lifting up Christ shall we draw men unto Him.

We now come to the reply of the bride. He has called her fair; wisely and well does she reply:

> Behold thou art fair, my beloved, yea, pleasant:
> Also our couch is green.
> The beams of our house are cedars,
> And our rafters are firs.

I am [but] a rose of Sharon,
A lily of the valleys.

The last words are often quoted as though they were the utterance of the Bridegroom, but we believe erroneously. The bride says in effect, "Thou callest me fair and pleasant, the fairness and pleasantness are Thine; I am but a wild flower, a lowly, scentless rose of Sharon (*i.e.*, the autumn crocus), or a lily of the valley."

To this the Bridegroom responds: "Be it so; but if a wild flower, yet

As a lily among thorns,
So is my love among the daughters."

Again the bride replies:

As the apple-tree [the citron] among the
trees of the wood,
So is my beloved among the sons.
I sat down under his shadow with great
delight,
And his fruit was sweet to my taste.

The citron is a beautiful evergreen, affording delightful shade as well as refreshing fruit. A humble wild flower herself, she recognizes her Bridegroom as a noble tree, alike ornamental and fruitful. Shade from the burning sun, refreshment and rest she finds in Him. What a contrast her present position and feelings to those with which

this section commenced! He knew full well
the cause of all her fears. Her distrust
sprang from her ignorance of Himself, so
He took her aside, and in the sweet intimacies of mutual love her fears and distrust
have vanished, like the mists of the morning
before the rising sun.

But now that she has learned to know
Him, she has a further experience of His
love. He is not ashamed to acknowledge
her publicly.

> He brought me to the banqueting house,
> And his banner over me was love.

The house of wine is now as appropriate
as the King's chambers were. Fearlessly
and without shame she can sit at His side
His acknowledged spouse, the bride of His
choice. Overwhelmed with His love she exclaims:

> Stay ye me with raisins, comfort me with
>   apples:
> For I am sick of love.
> His left hand under my head,
> And his right hand doth embrace me.

Now she finds the blessedness of being
possessed. No longer her own, heart-rest
is alike her right and her enjoyment; and
so the Bridegroom would have it.

> I adjure you, O daughters of Jerusalem,
> By the roes, and by the hinds of the field,

That ye stir not up nor wake My love,
Until she[1] please.

It is never by His will that our rest
in Him is disturbed.

You may always be abiding,
    If you will, at Jesus' side;
In the secret of His presence
    You may every moment hide.

There is no change in His love; He is
the same yesterday, today, and forever. To
us He promises, "I will never leave thee,
never fail thee, nor forsake thee," and His
earnest exhortation and command is,
"Abide in me, and I in you."

---

[1] The pronoun here and in chapter 3:5 and 8:4
should not be *he* as in the King James Version, nor
it as in the American Standard Version, but *she*.

SECTION II

Communion Broken—Restoration

Song of Solomon 2:8—3:5

"Therefore we ought to give the more earnest heed to the things that were heard, lest haply we drift away from them."
—Heb. 2:1 (R.V.).

At the close of the first section we left the bride satisfied and at rest in the arms of her Beloved, who had charged the daughters of Jerusalem not to stir up nor awaken His love until she please. We might well suppose that a union so complete, a satisfaction so full, would never be interrupted by failure on the part of the happy bride. But alas, the experience of most of us shows how easily communion with Christ may be broken, and how needful are the exhortations of our Lord to those who are indeed branches of the true Vine, and cleansed by the Word which He has spoken, to abide in Him. The failure is never on His side. "Lo, I am with you alway." But alas, the bride often forgets the exhortation addressed to her in Psalm 45:

> Hearken, O daughter, and consider, and
> > incline thine ear;
> Forget also thine own people, and thy
> > father's house;
> So shall the king greatly desire thy beauty:
> For he is thy lord; and worship thou him.

In this section the bride has drifted back from her position of blessing into a state of worldliness. Perhaps the very restfulness of her new-found joy made her feel too secure. Perhaps she thought that, so far as she was concerned, there was no need for the exhortation, "Little children, keep yourselves from idols." Or she may have thought that the love of the world was so thoroughly taken away that she might safely go back, and, by a little compromise on her part, she might win her friends to follow her Lord too. Perhaps she scarcely thought at all: glad that she was saved and free, she forgot that the current—the course of this world—was against her; and insensibly glided, drifted back to that position out of which she was called, unaware all the time of backsliding. It is not necessary, when the current is against us, to turn the boat's head down the stream in order to drift, or for a runner in a race to turn back in order to miss the prize.

Ah, how often the enemy succeeds, by one device or another, in tempting the be-

liever away from that position of entire
consecration to Christ in which alone the
fullness of His power and of His love can
be experienced. We say the fullness of His
power and of His love; for the believer
may not have ceased to love his Lord.

In the passage before us the bride still
loves Him truly, though not wholly. There
is still a power in His Word which is not
unfelt, though she no longer renders in-
stant obedience. She little realizes how she
is wronging her Lord, and how real is the
wall of separation between them. To her,
worldliness seems as but a little thing. She
has not realized the solemn truth of many
passages in the Word of God that speak
in no measured terms of the folly, the danger, the sin of friendship with the world.

> Love not the world, neither the things
> that are in the world. If any man love
> the world, the love of the Father is
> not in him.
> Ye adulteresses, know ye not that the
> friendship of the world is enmity with
> God? Whosoever therefore would be a
> friend of the world maketh himself an en-
> emy of God.
> Be not unequally yoked with unbe-
> lievers: for what fellowship have right-
> eousness and iniquity? or what com-
> munion hath light with darkness? And
> what concord hath Christ with Belial?

or what portion hath a believer with an
unbeliever? Wherefore, Come ye out from
among them, and be ye separate, saith
the Lord,
And touch no unclean thing;
And I will receive you,
And will be to you a Father,
And ye shall be to me sons and daughters,
    saith the Lord Almighty.

We have to take our choice: we cannot enjoy both the world and Christ.

The bride had not learned this: she
would fain enjoy both, with no thought of
their incompatibility. She observes with joy
the approach of the Bridegroom.

The voice of my beloved! Behold he cometh
Leaping upon the mountains, bounding
    over the hills.
My beloved is like a gazelle or a young hart;
Behold he standeth behind our wall,
He looketh in at the windows,
He glanceth through the lattice.

The heart of the bride leaps on hearing
the voice of her Beloved, as He comes in
search of her. He has crossed the hills.
He draws near to her. He stands behind
the wall. He even looks in at the windows.
With tender and touching words He woos
her to come forth to Him. He utters no
reproach, and His loving entreaties sink
deep in her memory.

My beloved spake, and said unto me,
Rise up, my love, my fair one, and come away.
For, lo, the winter is past,
The rain is over and gone;
The flowers appear on the earth;
The time of the singing of birds is come,
And the voice of the turtle is heard in our land;
The fig-tree ripeneth her green figs,
And the vines are in blossom,
They give forth their fragrance.
Arise, my love, my fair one, and come away.

All nature is responsive to the return of the summer; wilt thou, My bride, be irresponsive to My love?

Arise, my love, my fair one, and come away.

Can such pleading be in vain? Alas, it can. It was!

In yet more touching words the Bridegroom continues:

O my dove, that art in the clefts of the
    rock, in the covert of the steep place,
Let me see thy countenance, let me hear
    thy voice!
For sweet is thy voice, and thy countenance
    is comely.

Wonderful thought, that God should desire fellowship with us, and that He whose love once made Him the Man of Sorrows may now be made the Man of Joys by the loving devotion of human hearts!

But strong as is His love, and His desire

for His bride, He can come no farther.
Where she now is He can never come. But
surely she will go forth to Him. Has He
not a claim upon her? She feels and enjoys
His love; will she let His desire count for
nothing? For, let us notice, it is not here
the bride longing in vain for her Lord, but
the Bridegroom who is seeking for her.
Alas that He should seek in vain!

> Take us the foxes, the little foxes, that
>   spoil the vineyards;
> For our vineyards are in blossom,

He continues. The enemies may be small
but the mischief done great. A little spray
of blossom, so tiny as to be scarcely per-
ceived, is easily spoiled, but thereby the
fruitfulness of a whole branch may be forever destroyed. And how numerous the little foxes are! Little compromises with the
world, disobedience to the still small voice
in little things, little indulgences of the flesh
to the neglect of duty, little strokes of pol-
icy, doing evil in little things that good
many come, and the beauty and the fruitfulness of the vine are sacrificed!

We have a sad illustration of the deceit-
fulness of sin in the response of the bride.
Instead of bounding forth to meet Him,
she first comforts her own heart by the

remembrance of His faithfulness, and of her union with Him:

> My beloved is mine, and I am his:
> He feedeth *his flock* among the lilies.

My position is one of security. I have no need to be concerned about it. He is mine and I am His, and nought can alter that relationship. I can find Him now at any time; He feedeth His flock among the lilies. While the sun of prosperity shines upon me I may safely enjoy myself here without Him. Should trial and darkness come He will be sure not to fail me.

> Until the day be cool, and the shadows
>   flee away,
> Turn, my beloved, and be thou like a
>   gazelle or a young hart
> Upon the mountains of Bether.

Careless of His desire, she thus lightly dismisses Him, with the thought, "A little later I may enjoy His love," and the grieved Bridegroom departs!

Poor foolish bride! She will soon find that the things that once satisfied her can satisfy no longer; and that it is easier to turn a deaf ear to His tender call than to recall or find her absent Lord.

The day became cool, and the shadows did flee away, but He returned not. Then in the solemn night she discovered her mistake: it was dark, and she was alone. Retiring to rest she still hoped for His return—the lesson that worldliness is an absolute bar to full communion still unlearned.

> By night on my bed I sought him whom my
>   soul loveth:
> I sought him, but I found him not!

She waits and wearies. His absence becomes insupportable:

> *I said,* I will rise now, and go about the city,
> In the streets and in the broad ways,
> I will seek him whom my soul loveth:
> I sought him, but I found him not!

How different her position from what it might have been! Instead of seeking Him alone, desolate and in the dark, she might have gone forth with Him in the sunshine, leaning upon His arm. She might have exchanged the partial view of her Beloved through the lattice, when she could no longer say "Nothing between," for the joy of His embrace, and His public confession of her as His chosen bride!

> The watchmen that go about the city found
>   me:
> *To whom I said,* Saw ye him whom my
>   soul loveth?
> It was but a little that I passed from them,
> When I found him whom my soul loveth.

She had already obeyed His command,

"Arise, and come away." Fearless of reproach, she was seeking Him in the dark;
and when she began to confess her Lord
she soon found Him and was restored to
His favor:

> I held him, and would not let him go,
> Until I had brought him into my mother's
>   house,
> And into the chamber of her that conceived
>   me.

Jerusalem above is the mother of us
all. There it is that communion is enjoyed,
not in worldly ways or self-willed indul-
gence.

Communion fully restored, the section
closes, as did the first, with the loving
charge of the Bridegroom that none should
disturb His bride:

> I adjure you, O daughters of Jerusalem,
> By the roes, and by the hinds of the field,
> [By all that is loving and beautiful and
>   constant]
> That ye stir not up, nor awake My love,
> Until she[1] please.

May we all, while living down here, in
the world, but not of it, find our home in
the heavenly places to which we have been
raised, and in which we are seated together

---

[1] See footnote on page 35.

with Christ. Sent into the world to witness
for our Master, may we ever be strangers
there, ready to confess Him the true object
of our soul's devotion.

> How amiable are thy tabernacles,
> O Lord of hosts!
> My soul longeth, yea even fainteth for the
>   courts of the Lord;
> My heart and my flesh cry out unto the
>   living God.
> Blessed are they that dwell in thy house:
> They will be still praising thee. . . .
> A day in thy courts is better than a thousand.
> I had rather be a doorkeeper in the house
>   of my God
> Than to dwell in the tents of wickedness.
> For the Lord God is a sun and shield:
> The Lord will give grace and glory:
> No good thing will he withhold from them
>   that walk uprightly.
> O Lord of hosts,
> Blessed is the man that trusteth in thee.

SECTION III

The Joy of Unbroken Communion

Song of Solomon 3:6—5:1

O Jesus, King most wonderful,
    Thou Conqueror renown'd,
Thou sweetness most ineffable,
In whom all joys are found!
Thee, Jesus, may our voices bless;
    Thee may we love alone;
And ever in our lives express
    The image of Thine own.

We have been mainly occupied in Sections One and Two with the words and the experiences of the bride. In marked contrast to this, in this section our attention is first called to the Bridegroom, and then it is from Him that we hear of the bride, as the object of His love and the delight of His heart. The daughters of Jerusalem are the first speakers.

Who is this that cometh up out of the
    wilderness like pillars of smoke,
Perfumed with myrrh and frankincense,
With all powders of the merchant?

They themselves give the reply:

46

King Solomon made himself a car of state
Of the wood of Lebanon.
He made the pillars thereof of silver,
The bottom thereof of gold, the seat of it
    of purple,
The midst thereof being paved with love
    [love-gifts],
From the daughters of Jerusalem.

Behold, it is the litter of Solomon;
Threescore mighty men are about it,
Of the mighty men of Israel.
They all handle the sword, and are expert
    in war:
Every man hath his sword upon his thigh,
Because of fear in the night.

In these verses the bride is not mentioned; she is eclipsed in the grandeur and
the state of her royal Bridegroom; never-
theless, she is both enjoying and sharing
it. The very air is perfumed by the smoke
of the incense that ascends pillar-like to
the clouds, and all that safeguards the position of the Bridegroom Himself, and shows
forth His dignity, safeguards also the ac-
companying bride, the sharer of His glory.
The car of state in which they sit is built
of fragrant cedar from Lebanon, and the
finest of the gold and silver have been lav-
ished in its construction. The fragrant wood
typifies the beauty of sanctified humanity,

while the gold reminds us of the divine
glory of our Lord, and the silver of the
purity and preciousness of His redeemed
and peerless church. The imperial purple
with which it is lined tells us of the Gen-
tiles—the daughter of Tyre has been there
with her gift—while the love-gifts of the
daughters of Jerusalem accord with the
prophecy, "Even the rich among the people
shall intreat thy favor."

These are the things that attract the
attention of the daughters of Jerusalem,
but the bride is occupied with the King
Himself, and she exclaims:

> Go forth, O ye daughters of Zion, and be-
> hold King Solomon,
> With the crown wherewith his mother hath
> crowned him in the day of his espousals,
> And in the day of the gladness of his heart.

The crowned King is everything to her,
and she would have Him to be so to the
daughters of Zion likewise. She dwells with
delight on the gladness of His heart in the
day of His espousals, for now she is not
occupied with Him for her *own* sake, but
rejoices in His joy in finding in her *His*
satisfaction. Do we sufficiently cultivate
this unselfish desire to be all for Jesus,
and to do all for His pleasure? Or are
we conscious that we principally go to Him

for our own sakes, or at best for the sake
of our fellow creatures? How much of
prayer there is that begins and ends with
the creature, forgetful of the privilege of
giving joy to the Creator! Yet it is only
when He sees in our unselfish love and
devotion to Him the reflection of His own
that His heart can feel full satisfaction,
and pour itself forth in precious utterances
of love such as those which we find in the
following words:

> Behold, thou art fair, My love; behold,
>   thou art fair;
> Thine eyes are as dove's behind thy veil;
> Thy hair is as a flock of goats,
> That lie along the side of Mount Gilead;
> Thy teeth are like a flock of ewes that are
>   newly shorn,
> Which are come up from the washing.
> Which are all of them in pairs,
> And none is bereaved among them.
> Thy lips are like a thread of scarlet,
> And thy speech is comely, etc. (See verses
>   3-5.)

We have already found the explanation
of the fairness of the bride in her reflecting
like a mirror the beauty of the Bridegroom.
Well may He with satisfaction describe her
beauty while she is thus occupied with Himself! The lips that speak only of Him are
like a thread of scarlet; the mouth or speech

which has no word of self, or for self, is
comely in His sight.

How sweet His words of appreciation
and commendation were to the bride we
can well imagine, but her joy was too deep
for expression. She was silent in her love.
She would not *now* think of sending Him
away until the day be cool and the shadows
flee away.

Still less does the Bridegroom think of
finding His joy apart from His bride. He
says:

> Until the day be cool, and the shadows
>   flee away,
> I will get me to the mountain of myrrh,
> And to the hill of frankincense.

Separation never comes because of any
withdrawing on His part. He is always
ready for communion with a prepared heart,
and in this happy communion the bride
becomes even fairer, and more like to her
Lord. She is being progressively changed
into His image, from one degree of glory
to another, through the wondrous working
of the Holy Spirit, until the Bridegroom
can declare:

> Thou art all fair, my love;
> And there is no spot on thee.

And now she is *fit for service,* and to it

the Bridegroom woos her: she will not now misrepresent Him:

> Come with me from Lebanon, my bride,
> With me from Lebanon;
> Look from the top of Amana,
> From the top of Senir and Hermon,
> From the lions' dens,
> From the mountains of the leopards

"Come with Me." It is always so. When our Saviour says, "Go ye therefore and disciple all nations," He precedes it by, "All power is given unto Me," and follows it by, "Lo, I am with you alway." Or when, as here, He calls His bride to come, it is still "with Me," and it is *in connection with this loving invitation* that for the first time He changes the word "My love," for the still more endearing one, "My bride."

What are lions' dens when the Lion of the tribe of Judah is with us, or mountains of leopards, when He is at our side! "I will fear no evil, for thou art with me." On the other hand, it is while His own is thus facing dangers and toiling with Him in service, that He says:

> Thou hast ravished my heart, my sister,
>   my bride;
> Thou hast ravished my heart with one look
>   from thine eyes,
> With one chain of thy neck.

Is it not wonderful how the heart of our Beloved can be thus ravished with the love of one who is prepared to accept His invitation, and go forth with Him seeking to rescue the perishing! The marginal reading of the Revised Version is very significant: "Thou hast ravished My heart," or "Thou hast given me courage." If the Bridegroom's heart may be encouraged by the fidelity and loving companionship of his bride, it is not surprising that we may cheer and encourage one another in our mutual service. The Apostle Paul had a steep mountain of difficulty to climb when he was being led as a captive to Rome, not knowing the things that awaited him there, but when the brethren met him at the Appii Forum he thanked God and took courage. May we ever thus strengthen one another's hands in God!

But to resume. The Bridegroom cheers the toilsome ascents and the steep pathways of danger with sweet communications of His love:

How fair is thy love, my sister, my bride!
How much better is thy love than wine!
And the smell of thine ointments than all
    manner of spices!
Thy lips, O my bride, drop as the
    honeycomb:

Honey and milk are under thy tongue;
And the smell of thy garments is like
    the smell of Lebanon.
A garden shut up is my sister, my bride;
A spring shut up, a fountain sealed.
Thy shoots are a paradise of pomegranates,
    with precious fruits;
Henna with spikenard plants,
Spikenard and saffron,
Calamus and cinnamon, with all trees
    of frankincense;
Myrrh and aloes, with all the chief spices.
Thou art a fountain of gardens,
A well of living waters,
And flowing streams from Lebanon.

Engaged with the Bridegroom in seeking to rescue the perishing, the utterances of her lips are to Him as honey and the honey-comb, and figure is piled upon figure to express His satisfaction and joy. She is a garden full of precious fruits and delight-ful perfumes, but a garden enclosed; the fruit she bears may bring blessing to many, but the garden is for Himself alone; she is a fountain, but a spring shut up, a foun-tain sealed. And yet again she is a fountain of gardens, a well of living waters and flowing streams from Lebanon: she carries fertility and imparts refreshment wherever she goes; and yet it is all of Him and for Him.

The bride now speaks for the second time in this section. As her first utterance was of Him, so now her second is for Him; self is found in neither.

> Awake, O north wind; and come, thou
>   south;
> Blow upon my garden, that the spices
>   thereof may flow out.
> Let my beloved come into his garden,
> And eat his precious fruits.

She is ready for any experience: the north wind and the south may blow upon her garden, if only the spices thereof may flow out to regale her Lord by their fragrance. He has called her His garden, a paradise of pomegranates and precious fruits; let Him come into it and eat His precious fruits.

To this the Bridegroom replies:

> I am come into my garden, my sister,
>   my bride:
> I have gathered my myrrh with my spice;
> I have eaten my honeycomb with my honey;
> I have drunk my wine with my milk.

Now when she calls, He answers at once. When she is only for her Lord, He assures her that He finds all His satisfaction in her.

The section closes by the bride's invitation to His friends and hers, as well as to Himself:

Eat, O friends;
Drink, yea, drink abundantly, O beloved.

The consecration of all to our Master, far from lessening our power to impart, increases both our power and our joy in ministration. The five loaves and two fishes of the disciples, first given up to and blessed by the Lord, were abundant supply for the needy multitudes, and grew, in the act of distribution, into a store of which twelve hampers full of fragments remained when all were fully satisfied.

We have, then, in this beautiful section, as we have seen, a picture of unbroken communion and its delightful issues. May our lives correspond! First, one with the King, then speaking of the King; the joy of communion leading to fellowship in service, to a being all for Jesus, ready for any experience that will fit for further service, surrendering all to Him, and willing to minister all for Him. There is no room for love of the world here, for union with Christ has filled the heart. There is nothing for the gratification of the world, for all has been sealed and is kept for the Master's use.

Jesus, my life is Thine!
And evermore shall be
    Hidden in Thee.
For nothing can untwine
Thy life from mine.

SECTION IV

Communion Again Broken—Restoration

Song of Solomon 5:2—6:10

The fourth section commences with an address of the bride to the daughters of Jerusalem, in which she narrates her recent sad experience, and entreats their help in her trouble. The presence and comfort of her Bridegroom are again lost to her, not this time by relapse into worldliness, but by slothful self-indulgence.

We are not told of the steps that led to her failure, of how self again found place in her heart. Perhaps spiritual pride in the achievements which grace enabled her to accomplish was the cause. Or, not improbably, a cherished satisfaction in the *blessing* she had received, instead of in the Blesser Himself, may have led to the separation. She seems to have been largely unconscious of her declension. Self-occupied and self-contented, she scarcely noticed His absence. She was resting, resting alone— never asking where He had gone, or how He was employed. And more than this, the door of her chamber was not only closed, but barred—an evidence that His return was neither eagerly desired nor expected.

Yet her heart was not far from Him. There was a music in His voice that awakened echoes in her soul such as no other voice could have stirred. She was still "a garden shut up, a fountain sealed" so far as the world was concerned. The snare this time was the more dangerous and insidious because it was quite unsuspected. Let us look at her narrative:

> I was asleep, but my heart waked:
> It is the voice of my beloved that knock-
>   eth saying,
> Open to me, my sister, my love, my dove,
>   my undefiled:
> For my head is filled with dew,
> My locks with the drops of the night.

How often the position of the Bridegroom is that of a knocking Suitor outside, as in His epistle to the Laodicean[1] Church: "Behold, I stand at the door, and knock: if any man hear my voice, and open the door, I will come in to him, and will sup with him, and he with me." It is sad that He

---

[1] The Church of Popular Opinion, as pointed out by the Rev. Charles Fox in an address at Keswick, as the Church of Philadelphia is the Church of Brotherly Love.

should be outside a closed door—that He
should need to knock—but still more sad
that He should knock, and knock in vain
at the door of any heart which has become
His own. In this case it is not the *position*
of the bride that is wrong. If it were, His
word as before would be, "Arise, and come
away"; whereas now His word is, "Open
to Me, My sister, My love." It was her
condition of self-satisfaction and love of
ease that closed the door.

Very touching are His Words: "Open to
Me, My sister" (He is the first-born among
many brethren), "My love" (the object of
My heart's devotion), "My dove" (one who
has been endued with many of the gifts and
graces of the Holy Spirit), "My undefiled"
(washed, renewed, and cleansed for Me);
and He urges her to open by reference to
His own condition:

> My head is filled with dew,
> My locks with the drops of the night.

Why is it that His head is filled with the
dew? Because His heart is a shepherd-
heart. There are those whom the Father
has given to Him who are wandering on the
dark mountains of sin. Many, oh, how
many, have never heard the Shepherd's
voice. Many, too, who were once in the fold
have wandered away—far away from its

safe shelter. The heart that never can forget, the love that never can fail, *must* seek the wandering sheep until the lost one has been found. "My Father worketh hitherto, and I work." And will she, who so recently was at His side, who joyfully braved the dens of lions and the mountains of leopards, will she leave Him to seek alone the wandering and the lost?

> Open to me, my sister, my love, my dove,
> my undefiled:
> For my head is filled with dew,
> My locks with the drops of the night.

We do not know a more touching entreaty in the Word of God, and sad indeed is the reply of the bride:

> I have put off my coat; how shall I put it
> on?
> I have washed my feet; how shall I defile them?

How sadly possible it is to take delight in conferences and conventions, to feast on all the good things that are brought before us, and yet to be unprepared to go out from them to self-denying efforts to rescue the perishing; to delight in the rest of faith while forgetful to fight the good fight of faith; to dwell upon the cleansing and the purity effected by faith, but to have little thought for the poor souls struggling in the

mire of sin. If we can put off our coat when
He would have us keep it on, if we can
wash our feet while He is wandering alone
upon the mountains, is there not sad want
of fellowship with our Lord?

Meeting with no response from the tardy
bride, her

> Beloved put in his hand by the hole of
>   the door,
> And [her] heart was moved for him.

But, alas, the door was not only latched,
but barred; and His effort to secure an en-
trance was in vain.

> I rose up to open to my beloved;
> And my hands dropped with myrrh,
> And my fingers with liquid myrrh,
> Upon the handles of the bolt.
> I opened to my beloved;
> But my beloved had withdrawn himself,
>   and was gone.
> My soul had failed me when he spake.

When, all too late, the bride did arise,
she seems to have been more concerned
to anoint herself with the liquid myrrh than
to speedily welcome her waiting Lord, more
occupied with her own graces than with
His desire. No words of welcome were uttered, though her heart failed within her,
and the grieved One had withdrawn Himself
before she was ready to receive Him. Again

(as in the third chapter) she had to go forth
alone to seek her Lord, and this time her
experiences were much more painful than
on the former occasion.

> I sought him, but I could not find him;
> I called him, but he gave me no answer.
> The watchmen that go about the city found
> me,
> They smote me, they wounded me;
> The keepers of the walls took away my
> mantle from me.

Her first relapse had been one of inex-
perience. If a second relapse had been
brought about by inadvertence, she should
at least have been ready and prompt when
summoned to obey. It is not a little thing
to fall into the habit of being tardy in obedience, even in the case of a believer. In the
case of the unbeliever the final issue of disobedience is inexpressibly awful:

> Turn you at my reproof:
> Behold, I will pour out my Spirit unto you,
> I will make known my words unto you.
> Because I have called, and ye refused;
> I have stretched out my hand, and no man
> regarded; . . .
> I also will laugh in the day of your cala-
> mity. . . .
> Then shall they call upon me, but will I
> not answer;
> They shall seek me diligently, but they
> shall not find me.

The backsliding of the bride, though painful, was not final, for it was followed by true repentance. She went forth into the darkness and sought Him. She called, but He responded not, and the watchmen finding her, both smote and wounded her. They appear to have appreciated the gravity of her declension more correctly than she had done. Believers may be blinded to their own inconsistencies; others, however, note them, and the higher the position with regard to our Lord the more surely will any failure be visited with reproach.

Wounded, dishonored, unsuccessful in her search, and almost in despair, the bride turns to the daughters of Jerusalem and, recounting the story of her sorrows, adjures *them* to tell her Beloved that she is not unfaithful or unmindful of Him.

> I adjure you, O daughters of Jerusalem, if
>   ye find my beloved,
> That ye tell him, that I am sick of love.

The reply of the daughters of Jerusalem shows very clearly that the sorrow-stricken bride, wandering in the dark, is not recognized as the bride of the King, though her personal beauty does not escape notice.

> What is thy beloved more than another
>   beloved,
> O thou fairest among women?

> What is thy beloved more than another be-
>   loved,
> That thou dost so adjure us?

This question, implying that her Beloved
was no more than any other, stirs her soul
to its deepest depths and forgetting herself,
she pours out from the fullness of her heart
a soul-ravishing description of the glory
and beauty of her Lord.

> My beloved is white and ruddy,
> The chiefest among ten thousand.

(see verses 10-16, concluding with)

> His mouth is most sweet: yea, he is alto-
>   gether lovely.
> This is my beloved, and this is my friend,
> O daughters of Jerusalem.

It is interesting to compare the bride's
description of the Bridegroom with the de-
scriptions of the Ancient of Days in Daniel
7:9-10, and of our risen Lord in Revelation
1:13-16. The differences are very character-
istic.

In Daniel 7 we see the Ancient of Days
seated on the throne of judgment. His garment was white as snow, and the hair of
His head like the pure wool. His throne and
His wheels were as burning fire, and a fiery
stream issued and came forth from before
Him. The Son of Man was brought near be-

fore Him, and received from Him dominion,
and glory, and an everlasting kingdom that
shall not be destroyed. In Revelation 1 we
see the Son of Man Himself clothed with
a garment down to the foot, and His head
and His hair were white as wool, white as
snow; but the bride sees her Bridegroom
in all the vigor of youth, with locks "bushy,
and black as a raven." The eyes of the
risen Saviour are described as "a flame of
fire," but His bride sees them "like doves
beside the water brooks." In Revelation
"His voice is as the voice of many waters
. . . and out of His mouth proceeded a sharp
two-edged sword." To the bride, His lips
are as lilies, dropping liquid myrrh, and
His mouth most sweet. The countenance of
the risen Saviour was "as the sun shineth
in his strength," and the effect of the vision
on John—"when I saw Him, I fell at His
feet as one dead"—was not unlike the effect
of the vision given to Saul as he neared
Damascus. But to His bride, "His aspect
is like Lebanon, excellent as the cedars."
The Lion of the tribe of Judah is to His
own bride the King of love, and, with full
heart and beaming face, she so recounts
His beauties that the daughters of Jerusalem are seized with strong desire to seek
Him with her, that they also may behold
His beauty.

Whither is thy beloved gone,
O thou fairest among women?
Whither hath thy beloved turned him,
That we may seek him with thee?

The bride replies:

My beloved is gone down to his garden,
    to the beds of spices,
To feed in the gardens, and to gather lilies.
I am my beloved's, and my beloved is mine:
He feedeth his flock among the lilies.

Forlorn and desolate as she might appear, she still knows herself as the object of His affections, and claims Him as her own. This expression, "I am my Beloved's, and my Beloved is mine," is similar to that found in the second chapter, "My Beloved is mine, and I am His," yet with noteworthy difference. Then her first thought of Christ was of her claim upon Him: His claim upon her was secondary. Now she thinks first of His claim, and only afterward mentions her own. We see a still further development of grace in 7:10, where the bride, losing sight of her claim altogether, says:

I am my beloved's,
And his desire is toward me.

No sooner has she uttered these words and acknowledged herself as His rightful possession—a claim which she had practically repudiated when she kept Him barred

out—than her Bridegroom Himself appears. And with no upbraiding word, but
in tenderest love, tells her how beautiful
she is in His eyes, and speaks her praise
to the daughters of Jerusalem.

To her He says:

Thou art beautiful, O my love, as Tirzah,
    [the beautiful city of Samaria,]
Comely as Jerusalem,
    [the glorious city of the great King,]
Terrible [brilliant] as an army with banners.
Turn away thine eyes from Me,
For they have overcome Me. (See vv. 4-7.)

Then, turning to the daughters of Jerusalem, He exclaims:

There are threescore queens, and four-
    score concubines,
And maidens without number.
My dove, my perfect one, is but one;
She is the only one of her mother;
She is the choice one of her that bare her.
The daughters saw her, and called her
    blessed;
Yea, the queens and the concubines, and
    they praised her, saying,
Who is she that looketh forth as the morn-
    ing,
Fair as the moon,
Clear as the sun
Brilliant as an army with banners?

Thus the section closes with communion
fully restored, the bride reinstated and

openly acknowledged by the Bridegroom as His own peerless companion and friend. The painful experience through which the bride has passed has been fraught with lasting good, and we have no further indication of interrupted communion, but in the remaining sections find only joy and fruitfulness.

SECTION V

Fruits of Recognized Union

Song of Solomon 6:11—8:4

In the second and fourth sections of this book we found the communion of the bride broken—in the former by backsliding into worldliness, and in the latter through slothful ease and self-satisfaction. The present section, like the third, is one of unbroken communion. It is opened by the words of the bride:

I went down into the garden of nuts,
To see the green plants of the valley,
To see whether the vine budded.
And the pomegranates were in flower.
Or ever I was aware, my soul set me
Among the chariots of my willing people.

As in the commencement of Section Three, the bride, in unbroken communion with her Lord, was present though unmentioned until she made her presence evident by her address to the daughters of Zion, so also in this section the presence of the King is unnoted until He Himself addresses His bride. But she is one with her Lord

68

as she engages in His service! His promise,
"Lo, I am with you alway," is ever fulfilled
to her. He has no more to woo her to arise
and come away, to tell her that His "head
is filled with dew," His "locks with the
drops of the night," or to urge her if she
love Him to feed His sheep and care for
His lambs. Herself His garden, she does
not forget to tend it, nor keep the vine-
yards of others while her own is neglected.
With Him as well as *for* Him, she goes to
the garden of nuts. So thorough is the union
between them that many commentators
have felt difficulty in deciding whether the
bride or the Bridegroom was the speaker—
and really it is a point of little moment;
for, as we have said, both were there, and
of one mind, yet we believe we are right
in attributing these words to the bride, as
she is the one addressed by the daughters
of Jerusalem, and the one who speaks to
them in reply.

The bride and Bridegroom appear to
have been discovered by their willing
people while thus engaged in the happy
fellowship of fruitful service, and the bride,
before she was aware of it, found herself
seated among the chariots of her people
—*her* people as well as *His*.

The daughters of Jerusalem would fain call her back:

Return, return, O Shulammite;
Return, return, that we may look upon thee.

There is no question now as to who she is, nor why her Beloved is more than another beloved. He is recognized as King Solomon, and to her is given the same name, only in its feminine form, *Shulammite.*

Some have seen in these words, "Return, return," an indication of the rapture of the church and explain some parts of the subsequent context which appear inconsistent with this view, as resumptive rather than progressive. Interesting as is this thought, and well as it would explain the absence of *reference* to the King in the preceding verses, we are not inclined to accept it, but look on the whole song as progressive, and its last words as being equivalent to the closing words of Revelation: "Surely I come quickly. Amen. Even so, come, Lord Jesus." We do not therefore look upon the departure of the bride from her garden as being other than temporary.

The bride replies to the daughters of Jerusalem:

Why will ye look upon the Shulammite?

or, as in the King James Version,

What will ye see in the Shulamite?

In the presence of the King, she cannot
conceive why any attention should be paid
to her. As Moses, coming down from the
mount, was unconscious that his face shone
with a divine glory, so was it here with
the bride. But we may learn this very important lesson, that many who do not see
the beauty of the Lord will not fail to admire His reflected beauty in His bride.
The eager look of the daughters of Jerusalem surprised the bride, and she says,
"You might be looking upon the dance of
Mahanaim [the dance of two companies of
Israel's fairest daughters] instead of upon
one who has no claim for attention, save
that she is the chosen, though unworthy,
bride of the glorious King."

The daughters of Jerusalem have no
difficulty in replying to her question. Recognizing her as of royal birth—"O Prince's
daughter"—as well as of queenly dignity,
they describe in true and Oriental language
the tenfold beauties of her person. From
her feet to her head they see only beauty
and perfection. What a contrast to her state
by nature! Once from the sole of the foot
even unto the head was but wounds, and

bruises, and festering sores; now her feet
are shod with the preparation of the Gos-
pel of peace, and the very hair of the
head proclaims her a Nazarite indeed—the
King Himself is held captive in the tresses
thereof.

But One, more to her than the daughters
of Jerusalem, responded to her unaffected
question, "What will ye see in the Shulamite?" The Bridegroom Himself replies
to it:

> How fair and how pleasant art thou,
> O love, for delights!

He sees in her the beauties and the
fruitfulness of the tall and upright palm,
of the graceful and clinging vine, of the
fragrant and evergreen citron. Grace has
made her like the palm tree, the emblem
alike of uprightness and of fruitfulness.
The fruit of the date-palm is more valued
than bread by the Oriental traveler, so
great is its sustaining power. The fruit-
bearing powers of the tree do not pass
away; as age increases the fruit becomes
more perfect as well as more abundant.

> The righteous shall flourish like the palm-
> tree:
> He shall grow like a cedar in Lebanon.
> They that are planted in the house of the
> Lord
> Shall flourish in the courts of our God.

> They shall still bring forth fruit in old age;
> They shall be full of sap and green.

But why are the righteous made so upright and flourishing?

> To show that the Lord is upright;
> He is my Rock, and there is no unrighteousness in Him.

One with our Lord, it is ours to *show forth* His graces and virtues, to reflect His beauty, to be His faithful witnesses.

The palm is also the emblem of victory. It raises its beautiful crown toward the heavens, fearless of the heat of the sultry sun or of the burning hot wind from the desert. From its beauty it was one of the ornaments of Solomon's, as it is to be of Ezekiel's temple. When our Saviour was received at Jerusalem as the King of Israel the people took branches of palm trees and went forth to meet Him; and in the glorious day of His espousals, a great multitude which no man can number, of all nations, and kindreds, and people, and tongues, shall stand before the throne and before the Lamb, clothed with white robes, and with palms of victory in their hands shall ascribe their salvation to our God which sitteth upon the throne, and unto the Lamb.

But if she resembles the palm she also resembles the vine. Much she needs the culture of the Husbandman, and well does she repay it. Abiding in Christ, the true source of fruitfulness, she brings forth clusters of grapes, luscious and refreshing, as well as sustaining, like the fruit of the palm—luscious and refreshing to Himself, the owner of the vineyard, as well as to the weary, thirsty world in which He has placed it.

The vine has its own suggestive lessons: it needs and seeks support; the sharp knife of the pruner often cuts away unsparingly its tender garlands and mars its appearance, while increasing its fruitfulness. It has been beautifully written:

> The living Vine, Christ chose it for Himself:
> God gave to man for use and sustenance
> Corn, wine, and oil, and each of these is
>   good:
> And Christ is Bread of life and Light of life.
> But yet, He did not choose the summer corn,
> That shoots up straight and free in one
>   quick growth,
> And has its day, is done, and springs no
>   more;
> Nor yet the olive, all whose boughs are
>   spread
> In the soft air, and never lose a leaf,
> Flowering and fruitful in perpetual peace;
> But only this, for Him and His is one—
> That everlasting, ever-quickening Vine,

That gives the heat and passion of the
    world,
Through its own life-blood, still renewed
    and shed.

The Vine from every living limb bleeds
    wine;
Is it the poorer for that spirit shed?
The drunkard and the wanton drink thereof;
Are they the richer for that gift's excess?
Measure thy life by loss instead of gain;
Not by the wine drunk, but the wine poured
    forth;
For love's strength standeth in love's
    sacrifice;
And whoso suffers most, hath most to give.

Yet one figure more is used by the Bridegroom: "The smell of thy breath [is] like
apples [citrons]." In the first section the
bride exclaims:

As the citron-tree among the trees of the
    wood,
So is my beloved among the sons.
I delighted and sat down under his shadow,
And his fruit was sweet to my taste.

Here we find the outcome of that communion. The citrons on which she had fed
perfumed her breath, and imparted to her
their delicious odor. The Bridegroom con-
cludes his description:

Thy mouth [is] like the best wine,
That goeth down smoothly—
For my beloved—

interjects the bride,

> Causing the lips of those that are asleep to
> move.

How wondrous the grace that has made the bride of Christ to be all this to her Beloved! Upright as the palm, victorious, and evermore fruitful as she grows heavenward; gentle and tender as the Vine, self-forgetful and self-sacrificing, not merely bearing fruit in spite of adversity, but bearing her richest fruits through it; feasting on her Beloved, as she rests beneath His shade, and thereby partaking of His fragrance—what has grace not done for her! And what must be her joy in finding, ever more fully, the satisfaction of the glorious Bridegroom in the lowly wild flower He has made His bride, and beautified with His own graces and virtues!

> I am my beloved's,
> And his desire is toward me,

she gladly exclaims. Now it is none of self or for self, but all of Thee and for Thee. And if such be the sweet fruits of going down to the garden of nuts, and caring for His garden with Him, she will need no constraining to continue in this blessed service.

> Come, my beloved, let us go forth into the
> field;
> Let us lodge in the villages.

She is not ashamed of her lowly origin, for she fears no shame. Perfect love has cast out fear. The royal state of the King, with its pomp and grandeur, may be enjoyed by and by: now, more sweet with Him at her side to make the garden fruitful; to give to Him all manner of precious fruits, new and old, which she has laid up in store for Him; and best of all to satisfy Him with her own love. Not only is she contented with this fellowship of service, but she could fain wish that there were no honors and duties to claim His attention, and for the moment to lessen the joy of His presence.

> Oh that thou wert as my brother,
> That sucked the breasts of my mother!
> When I should find thee without, I would
>   kiss thee;
> Yea, and none would despise me.

Would that she could care for Him, and claim His whole attention, as a sister might care for a brother. She is deeply conscious that He has richly endowed her, and that she is as nothing compared with Him. But instead of proudly dwelling upon what she has done through Him, she would fain that it were possible for her to be the giver and Him the receiver. Far removed is this from the grudging thought, that must so grate upon the heart of our Lord, "I do not think that God requires this of me"; or, "Must I give up that, if I am to be a Christian?" True devotion will rather ask to be allowed to give, and will count as loss all which may not be given up for the Lord's sake. "I count all things but loss, for the excellency of the knowledge of Christ Jesus my Lord."

This longing desire to be more to Him does not, however, blind her to the consciousness that she needs His guidance, and that He is her true, her only Instructor.

> I would lead thee, and bring thee into
>   my mother's house,
> That thou mightest instruct me;
> I would cause thee to drink of spiced wine,
> Of the juice of my pomegranate.

I would give Thee my best, and yet would myself seek all my rest and satisfaction in Thee.

> His left hand should be under my head,
> And His right hand should embrace me.

And thus the section closes. There is nothing sweeter to the Bridegroom or to the bride than this hallowed and unhindered communion. And again He adjures the daughters of Jerusalem, in slightly different form:

> Why should ye stir up, or why awake my
>   love,
> Until she[1] please?

Hallowed communion indeed! May we ever enjoy it and, abiding in Christ, we shall sing, in the familiar words of the well-known hymn—

> Both Thine arms are clasped around me,
>   And my head is on Thy breast;
> And my weary soul hath found Thee
>   Such a perfect, perfect rest!
>   Blessed Jesus,
> Now I know that I am blest.

---

[1] See footnote on page 35.

SECTION VI

Unrestrained Communion

Song of Solomon 8:5-14

We have now reached the closing section of this book, which, as we have seen, is a poem describing the life of a believer on earth. Beginning in Section One (1:2—2:7) with the unsatisfied longings of an espoused one—longings which could only be met by her unreserved surrender to the Bridegroom of her soul—we find that when the surrender was made, instead of the cross she had so much feared she found a King, the King of Love, who both satisfied her deepest longings, and found His own satisfaction in her.

The second section (2:8—3:5) showed failure on her part. She was lured back again into the world, and soon found that her Beloved could not follow her there. Then with full purpose of heart going forth to seek Him and confessing His name, her search was successful and her communion was restored.

The third section (3:6—5:1) told of unbroken communion. Abiding in Christ, she was the sharer of His security and His glory. She draws the attention, however, of the daughters of Jerusalem from these outward things to her King Himself. And, while she is thus occupied with Him, and would have others so occupied, she finds that her royal Bridegroom is delighting in her and inviting her to fellowship of service, fearless of dens of lions and mountains of leopards.

The fourth section (5:2—6:10), however, shows again failure; not as before through worldliness, but rather through spiritual pride and sloth. Restoration now was much more difficult, but again when she went forth diligently to seek her Lord and so confessed Him as to lead others to long to find Him with her, He revealed Himself and the communion was restored, to be interrupted no more.

The fifth section (6:11—8:4), as we have seen, describes not only the mutual satisfaction and delight of the bride and Bridegroom in each other, but the recognition of her position and her beauty by the daughters of Jerusalem.

And now in the sixth section (8:5-14) we come to the closing scene of the book. In it the bride is seen leaning upon her Be-

loved, asking Him to bind her yet more
firmly to Himself, and occupying herself in
His vineyard, until He calls her away from
earthly service. To this last section we shall
now give our attention more particularly.

It opens, as did the third, by an inquiry
or exclamation of the daughters of Jerusalem. There they asked, "Who is this that
cometh out of the wilderness like pillars of
smoke? . . ." but then their attention was
claimed by the pomp and state of the King,
not by His person, nor by that of His bride.
Here they are attracted by the happy position of the bride in relation to her Beloved,
and not by their surroundings.

> Who is this that cometh up from the
>   wilderness,
> Leaning upon her beloved?

It is through the bride that attention is
drawn to the Bridegroom; their union and
communion are now open and manifest. For
the last time the wilderness is mentioned;
but sweetly solaced by the presence of the
Bridegroom, it is *no wilderness to the bride.*
In all the trustfulness of confiding love she
is seen leaning upon her Beloved. He is her
strength, her joy, her pride, and her prize,
while she is His peculiar treasure, the object of His tenderest care. All His resources
of wisdom and might are hers; though jour-

neying she is at rest, though in the wilderness she is satisfied, while leaning upon her Beloved.

Wonderful, however, as are the revelations of grace and love to the heart taught by the Holy Spirit through the relationship of bride and Bridegroom, the Christ of God is more than Bridegroom to His people. He who when on earth was able to say, "Before Abraham was, I am," here claims His bride from her very birth, and not alone from her espousals. Before she knew Him, He knew her, and of this He reminds her in the words:

> I raised thee up under the citron-tree;
> There thy mother brought thee forth.

He takes delight in her beauty, but that is not so much the cause as the effect of His love, for He took her up when she had no comeliness. The love that has made her what she is, and now takes delight in her, is not a fickle love, nor need she fear its change.

Gladly does the bride recognize this truth, that she is indeed His own, and she exclaims:

> Set me as a seal upon thine heart, as a seal
>   upon thine arm:
> For love is strong as death;
> Jealousy [ardent love] is cruel [retentive]
>   as the grave;

The flashes thereof are flashes of fire,
A very flame of the Lord.

The High Priest bore the names of the
twelve tribes upon his heart, each name being engraved as a seal in the costly and
imperishable stone chosen by God, each
seal or stone being set in the purest gold;
he likewise bore the same names upon his
shoulders, indicating that both the love and
the strength of the High Priest were pledged
on behalf of the tribes of Israel. The bride
would be thus upborne by Him who is alike
her Prophet, Priest, and King, for love is
strong as death, and jealousy, or ardent
love, retentive as the grave. Not that she
doubts the constancy of her Beloved, but
that she has learned, alas, the incon-
stancy of her own heart, and she would be
bound to the heart and arm of her Beloved
as with chains and settings of gold, even
the emblem of deity. Thus the Psalmist
prayed, "Bind the sacrifice with cords,
even unto the horns of the altar."

It is comparatively easy to lay the sacrifice on the altar that sanctifies the gift,
but it requires divine compulsion—the
cords of love—to retain it there. So here
the bride would be set and fixed on the heart
and on the arm of Him who is henceforth
to be her all in all, that she may evermore

trust only in that love, be sustained only
by that power.

Do we not all need to learn a lesson from
this? and to pray to be kept from turning
to Egypt for help, from trusting in horses
and chariots, from putting confidence in
princes, or in the son of man, rather than
in the living God? How the kings of Israel,
who had won great triumphs by faith, sometimes turned aside to heathen nations in
their later years! The Lord keep His people from this snare.

The bride continues: "The flashes of
love are flashes of fire, a very flame of the
Lord." It is worthy of note that this is the
only occurrence of the word "Lord" in this
book. But how could it be omitted here?
For love is of God, and God is love.

To her request the Bridegroom replies
with reassuring words:

Many waters cannot quench love,
Neither can the floods drown it:
If a man would give all the substance of his
    house for love,
It would utterly be contemned.

The love which grace has begotten in the
heart of the bride is itself divine and per-
sistent; many waters cannot quench it, nor
the floods drown it. Suffering and pain, be-
reavement and loss may test its constancy,

but they will not quench it. Its source is
not human or natural. Like the life, it is
hidden with Christ in God. What "shall
separate us from the love of Christ? shall
tribulation, or distress, or persecution, or
famine, or nakedness, or peril, or sword?
... Nay, in all these things we are more
than conquerors through Him that loved us.
For I am persuaded that neither death, nor
life, nor angels, nor principalities, nor powers, nor things present, nor things to come,
nor height, nor depth, nor any other crea-
tion [A.R.V. margin], shall be able to separate us from the love of God, which is in
Christ Jesus our Lord." Our love to God
is secured by God's love to us. To the soul
really rescued by grace, no bribe to forsake
God's love will be finally successful. "If a
man would give all the substance of his
house for love, it would utterly be contemned."

Freed from anxiety on her own account,
the happy bride next asks guidance, and
fellowship in service with her Lord, on behalf of those who have not yet reached her
favored position.

> We have a little sister,
> And she hath no breasts:
> What shall we do for our sister
> In the day when she shall be spoken for?

How beautifully her conscious union with the Bridegroom appears in her expressions. "*We* have a little sister," not *I* have, etc.; "what shall *we* do for our sister?" etc. She has neither private relationships nor interests; in all things she is one with Him. And we see a further development of grace in the very question. Toward the close of the last section she recognized the Bridegroom as her Instructor. She will not now make her own plans about her little sister, and ask His acquiescence in them. She will rather learn what His thoughts are, and have fellowship with Him in His plans.

How much anxiety and care the children of God would be spared if they learned to act in this way! Is it not too common to make the best plans that we can, and to carry them out as best we may, feeling all the while a great burden of responsibility, and earnestly asking the Lord to help *us*? Whereas if we always let *Him* be our Instructor in service, and leave the responsibility with *Him*, our strength would not be exhausted with worry and anxiety, but all would be at His disposal, and accomplish His ends.

In the little sister, as yet immature, may we not see the elect of God, given to Christ in God's purpose, but not yet brought into saving relation to Him? And perhaps also those babes in Christ who as yet need feeding with milk and not with meat, but who, with such care, will in due time become experienced believers, fitted for the service of the Lord? Then they will be spoken for, and called into that department of service for which He has prepared them.

The Bridegroom replies:

> If she be a wall,
> We will build upon her battlements of silver;
> And if she be a door,
> We will inclose her with boards of cedar.

In this reply the Bridegroom sweetly recognizes His oneness with His bride, in the same way as she has shown her conscious oneness with Him. As she says, "What shall *we* do for our sister?" so He replies, "*We* will build . . . *we* will inclose," etc. He will not carry out His purposes of grace irrespective of His bride, but will work with and through her. What can be done for this sister, however, will depend upon what she becomes. If she be a wall, built upon the true foundation, strong and stable, she shall be adorned and beautified with battlements of silver. But if unstable and easily moved to and fro like a door, such treatment will be as impossible as unsuitable—she will need to be enclosed with boards of cedar, hedged in with restraints for her own protection.

The bride rejoicingly responds, "I am a wall." She knows the foundation on which she is built. There is no *if* in her case. She is conscious of having found favor in the eyes of her Beloved. Naphtali's blessing is hers: she is "satisfied with favor, and full with the blessing of the Lord."

But what is taught by the connection of this happy consciousness with the lines which follow?

> Solomon had a vineyard at Baal-hamon;
> He let out the vineyard unto keepers;
> Every one for the fruit thereof was to bring
>   a thousand pieces of silver.
> My vineyard, which is mine, is before me;
> Thou, O Solomon, shalt have the thousand,
> And those that keep the fruit thereof two
>   hundred.

The connection is, we believe, one of great importance, teaching us that what she *was* (by grace) was more important than what she *did*, and that she did not work in order to earn favor, but being assured of favor, gave her love free scope to show itself in service. The bride knew her relationship to her Lord, and His love to her. And in her determination that He should have the thousand pieces of silver, her concern was that her vineyard should not produce

less for her Solomon than His vineyard at
Baal-hamon. Her vineyard was herself, and
she desired for her Lord much fruit. She
would see too that the keepers of the vineyard, those who were her companions in
its culture, and who ministered in word and
doctrine, were well rewarded. She would
not muzzle the ox that treadeth out the corn.
A full tithe, nay a double tithe, was to be
the portion of those who kept the fruit and
labored with her in the vineyard.

How long this happy service continues,
and how soon it is to be terminated, we cannot tell. He who calls His servants to dwell
in the gardens, and cultivate them for Him
—as Adam of old was placed in the Paradise
of God—it is He alone who knows the limit
of this service. Sooner or later the rest will
come, the burden and heat of the last day
will have been borne, the last conflict will
be over, and the voice of the Bridegroom
will be heard addressing His loved one:

> Thou that dwellest in the gardens,
> The companions hearken to thy voice:
> Cause me to hear it.

Thy service among the companions is
finished. Thou hast fought the good fight,
thou hast kept the faith, thou hast finished
thy course; henceforth there is laid up for
thee the crown of righteousness, and the

Bridegroom Himself shall be thine exceeding great reward!

Well may the bride let Him hear her voice, and, springing forth in heart to meet Him, cry:

> Make haste, my beloved,
> And be thou like to a roe or to a young
> hart
> Upon the mountains of spices!

She no longer asks Him, as in the second section:

> Turn, my beloved, and be thou like a roe
> or a young hart
> Upon the mountains of Bether [separation].

She has never again wished Him to turn away from her, for there are no mountains of Bether to those who are abiding in Christ; now there are mountains of spices. He who inhabits the praises of Israel, which rise like the incense of spices from His people's hearts, is invited by His bride to make haste, to come quickly, and be like a roe or young hart upon the mountains of spices.

Very sweet is the presence of our Lord, as by His Spirit He dwells among His people, while they serve Him below. But here there are many thorns in every path, which call for watchful care, and it is meet that now we should suffer with our Lord in order that we may hereafter be glorified together.

The day is coming, however, in which He will bring us up out of the earthly gardens and associations to the palace of the great King. There His people "shall hunger no more, neither thirst any more; neither shall the sun light on them, nor any heat. For the Lamb, which is in the midst of the throne, shall feed them, and shall lead them unto living fountains of waters; and God shall wipe away all tears from their eyes."

> The Spirit and the bride say, Come! . . .
> Surely I come quickly.
> Amen; even so, come, Lord Jesus!

APPENDIX

The Daughters of Jerusalem

The question is frequently asked, Who are represented by the daughters of Jerusalem?

They are clearly not the bride, yet they are not far removed from her. They know where the Bridegroom makes His flock to rest at noon; they are charged by the Bridegroom not to stir up nor awaken His love when she rests, abiding in Him. They draw attention to the Bridegroom as with dignity and pomp He comes up from the wilderness. Their love-gifts adorn His chariot of state. They are appealed to by the bride for help in finding her Beloved and, stirred by her impassioned description of His beauty, they desire to seek Him with her. They describe very fully the beauty of the bride, but on the other hand we never find them occupied with the *person* of the Bridegroom; *He* is not all in all to them; they mind outward and earthly things.

Do they not represent those who are for the present more concerned about the

things of this world than the things of God?
To advance their own interests and to secure their own comfort concerns them more
than to be in all things pleasing to the Lord.
They *may* form part of that great company
spoken of in Revelation 7:9-17, who come
out of the great tribulation, but they will
not form part of the 144,000, "the first-
fruits unto God and to the Lamb" (Rev. 14:
1-5). They have forgotten the warning of our
Lord in Luke 21:34-36, and hence they are
not "accounted worthy to escape all these
things that shall come to pass, and to stand
before the Son of Man." They have not, with
Paul, counted "all things but loss for the
excellency of the knowledge of Christ Jesus
the Lord."

We wish to place on record our solemn
conviction that not all who are called Chris-
tians, or think themselves to be such, will
attain to that resurrection of which St. Paul
speaks in Philippians 3:11, or will thus meet
the Lord in the air. Unto those who by lives
of consecration manifest that they are not
of the world, but are looking for Him, He
will appear without sin unto salvation.